THE POWER TO
CHANGE GEOGRAPHY

Dear Ruth:

Fragments of your
finely honed poetry
and glimpses of your
lovely expressive face
keep drifting across
the back of my mind.
I hope we see each
other again soon.

     Much love,
     Diana

PRINCETON SERIES OF CONTEMPORARY POETS
David Wagoner, editorial adviser

OTHER BOOKS IN THE SERIES

Returning Your Call, *by Leonard Nathan*
Sadness And Happiness, *by Robert Pinsky*
Burn Down the Icons, *by Grace Schulman*
Reservations, *by James Richardson*
The Double Witness: Poems, *by Ben Belitt*
Night Talk and Other Poems, *by Richard Pevear*
Listeners at the Breathing Place, *by Gary Miranda*

THE POWER
TO CHANGE
GEOGRAPHY

Diana Ó Hehir

PRINCETON UNIVERSITY PRESS
PRINCETON, NEW JERSEY

Published by Princeton University Press, Princeton, New Jersey
In the United Kingdom: Princeton University Press, Guildford, Surrey

Library of Congress Cataloging in Publication Data will be
found on the last printed page of this book

Publication of this book has been aided by a grant from the Paul
Mellon Fund of Princeton University Press

This book has been composed in VIP Optima

Clothbound editions of Princeton University Press books
are printed on acid-free paper, and binding materials are
chosen for strength and durability.

Printed in the United States of America by Princeton
University Press, Princeton, New Jersey

Designed by Laury A. Egan

ACKNOWLEDGMENTS

Of the poems in this collection, "The Sea Creature" appeared in *Antaeus*; "Recovering" in *Brahma*; "Learning to Type" in *Berkeley Poetry Review*; "January Class: It Hasn't Rained in Seven Months" appeared in *Columbia*; "Living on the Earthquake Fault," "New Tenants," "An Isthmus in the Bay," "Metamorphosis," "Waterfall," and "The Power to Change Geography" appeared in *Kayak*. "In the Basement of my First House," "Victim," "Beseiged," "Returned in a Dream," "Night's End," "Watching," "The Worst Motel," "Waiting," "Four A.M.," "Are You Concerned for Your Safety, Alone in the House?" and "Exorcising Ghosts" appeared in *Poetry Northwest*; "Alone by the Road's Edge" in *Shenandoah*; "Maude's Bar," "I Attend the Saint's Death," "How to Forgive," and "Reprieved" in *Southern Poetry Review*. In addition, "Anima" has been accepted for publication by *Kayak*.

"Night's End" was one of a group of three poems which received *Poetry Northwest*'s Helen Bullis Award for 1976.

Some of these poems were first printed in a slightly different form.

Energy is the only life, and is from the body; and Reason is the bound or outward circumference of Energy.
Energy is eternal delight.

William Blake,
The Marriage of Heaven and Hell, 1790

TABLE OF CONTENTS

I

3   They Arrive This Morning
4   The Power to Change Geography
5   The Retarded Children Find a World Built Just for Them
6   The Prophet of Salt Lake City
7   Called
8   Vision: Fire Underground
9   I Attend the Saint's Death
10 Waterfall

II

13 The Days Are Getting Shorter
14 Alone by the Road's Edge
15 A Landscape Never Explored
16 Vision of Bea
17 In Mexico: The Indian Woman
18 We Live in the Ice Country
19 Survivor
20 Threatened
21 Victim
22 Illinois Central Hospital
23 The Sea Creature
24 House
25 The Child at the End of the World

III

29 Living on the Earthquake Fault
30 Growing Coal
31 The Worst Motel
32 Besieged
33 Cars Go By Outside, One After Another

34 An Isthmus in the Bay
35 Maude's Bar
36 Are You Concerned for your Safety, Alone in the House
37 Ship Wreck
38 January Class: It Hasn't Rained for Seven Months

IV

41 In the Basement of my First House
42 Recluse
43 Four A M
44 Our World, and Us, Remade by Heat
45 Metastasis
46 Anger
47 Waiting for my Eyes to Open on Day
48 Night's End
49 The Place Where Dreams Stop
50 New Tenants

V

53 After the Cataclysm
54 Watching
55 How to Forgive
56 Metamorphosis
57 Recovering
58 Exorcising Ghosts
59 Learning to Type
60 Reprieved
61 After You're All in Bed
62 Home
63 Anima

They Arrive This Morning

Those invaders from space will set down in a blue light, climb out of their
Pale machine carrying their charts, globes,
Maps of the rivers of the heart, their diagrams showing
That country we all long for.

It's lodged in the pit of the belly,
In that network of veins inside the head,
The knot at the back of the throat.
We ask: What color is the star that never sets?

Alone in your room at night, are you fearful, do you miss me; is
The skin of your knuckles pulled white;

Do you wait for them as I do? They have mirrors to lighten our waiting;
                                        elixirs that heal blindness;
They'll show us their tour of the body's skies
With its final, eradicable
Seat of loneliness.

Will they get here before daylight?
Will they reach us in time?

The Power to Change Geography

For all the ungainly ones, the awkward, silent ones, for
The pinched faces,
The hand trying to hold no shape, for that smile
That means: Wait for me, for corridors
Without doorways, walkways,
For all my other treasons, for the times I didn't return in time

Someone forgive me, absolve me, let me
Try to regain my light

That hovers still at the edge of my fingertips, walks up my arm, is of no use
To me only.

You sat in your chair with your head lowered,
You said my name without belief,
There was a tan plastic bandage over both your eyes,
I wanted to burn for you.

But the force lay behind me elusive as electricity, silent as sunshine,
Colorless, transparent,
Hovering outside of me,
Waiting to be summoned,
Promising
To take a shape.

The Retarded Children Find a World Built Just for Them

The doors of that city are ninety feet high,
On their panels are frescoes of ships, of mountains.

Inside is the children's kingdom
Where the mad ones, the foot-draggers, garglers,

Askew as a tower of beads,
Are sustained by the air. Buildings, like great gold chains

Emboss themselves around
The crazy children, their jewels.

The children turn and turn like dancers,
Their sweaters whirl out at their waists, their long chopped hair

Scrapes the sides of the archways,
They're happy, they're famous.

They walk on the streets in crystal shoes, lapis flows in the gutters;
Around the edge of each building there's a scarlet halo.

And those children with eyes like scars, with tongues sewed to the
                    roofs of their palates, with hands that jerk

Like broken-backed squirrels,
Feed the writing of light from the buildings;

They forgive us ninety times over;
They sing and sing like all the birds of the desert.

The Prophet of Salt Lake City

Who loved as frantically as I do,
Who stacked up his needs in a column of God's wrath,
Lifting against our light his arrogant power
Of certainty.

His wives nestled around him, soft as cushions,
They dug in his garden,
Wore kerchiefs to screen out the salty light; they raised
Children in his garden, and that's what did him in,
The slow march down the foothills

Muting his panic that might take the roof off of the world
And let in the noise that's out there.

He planned to touch that,
Out of his desert tower; he'd stand on the top
And drag the sky around his feet in shreds.

The salt hurts like old ambition, it makes
Ice on the tongue; it tastes
Even now, of prophecy.

Called

By earthquake, two pale tremors, wings closed,
By the city over the water,
Called by the rainless month. The city glitters like sand,
By solitude, by the voice that lives in air,
By view, trees, street on street scrubbed clean by wind,
By the sun arcing slowly over the dark gray marble.

Called by the god. Drawn out of space to the place where she is, curved
                                            against her shell of sky,
Face, forehead hidden in air;
All I can see is the bottom of her chin,
White column of throat, the hollow at its base, arm upraised to slit clouds.
                                            The eyes are golden skins
Burning a corner in sun.

Called without petition. Here's the step where I must go down,
Over the edge of the cleft in ground
Entering smoke that reeks of the world's core, of melted rock.

I draw it deep into me, carry it slowly,
Searing my lungs.

Vision; Fire Underground

Move across the grass like a shadow, out to the walk, down to the car,
Day pulling at your feet, and then
The sidewalk will open for you; at the bottom
Of its vast gorge, red, pearled, slippery,
Is a light most piercing, seam of diamonds, colors pulsing

Words across the bands of your eyes.

Blind as Paul, grope one by one for the trees,
Their bark grainy under your fingertips.

Where has it been taken now, that
Withheld breath, terrible chasm,
Heat to simmer the ends of the hair to crystal wire, turn the mind into
Its own molten country?

Neither pain nor solace but a vast opening in the air,
It listens across an ordinary day,
Grows fiery letters, waits

I Attend the Saint's Death

Noise descends on us like tents,
Beats in our eardrums with shrieks of windstorms, trains,
The round gray paving stones are slippery with hate.
The saint is arched, rigid as a roof brace,
Feet digging against mine in the stack of twigs, eyes search the sky

Where her name is written: shreds, ripped flags of ice
Shape her word
Its edges turning.

Since she was eleven, wheels in the troubled air;
The eye of purpose held her inside its camera.

She reaches for my memories;
Grasps at the freckled hand the child held,
Jostles against me on the rocking chair,
Wiry ribs that God has spoken to.

I tell her that I can't bear,
I leave her, my back smeared with fire, marked by calls that rock the air,
                                                            tear

Open the shield between her and the crowd.

She sees them, empty shapes upon each other; behind them, rims of
                                                    buildings;

After that is space,

A view that makes music of her raucous end,
And draws her down like rain.

Waterfall

Over the cliff, down an endless slope
Into the fall obscured by spray; nothing can hold it.

You with your good intentions,
Patting the edges of the clay banks, building dams,
Smiling wistfully, hopefully, poking
Things together, aiming a finger at them, saying: stick.

Water grinds down the mill of the cliff in surges, picks up
All the relics of our past: tokens, rings,
Artifacts painted blue,
They float, frantically, buoyantly, downhill.

Whatever I clutch will be swept away.
The tide's impartial; it roars change,
Roars foam like the side of a granite building, clusters of spray,
                                        water-smoke,
A tower higher than Babel, oblong, with shining sides.

The faces of all my people move in those colors;
Their hands in spray reach beyond me; their eyes look to the crest of the
                                        water; I'm
Drenched from head to foot;

My ears are filled with roaring.

II

The Days Are Getting Shorter

You make your own ending, my friend had said.
She stood on the edge of emptiness that traveled down to China;
Along its ridge her footsteps
Would stay a clear etching:
Here's the way you walk on the edge of a cliff,
And falling can happen well, it can be your own ending.

She said: there was a shape like a water-flower;
It opened until it filled my glass.

I think of her blue eyes, a color
That wedges itself home.

Comets crease my night this year; I saw
A fountain of fire rise vacillating over the city dump;
Pieces revolved down, behind me the trees were severe;
Ladies in play clothes tell me their breasts hurt,
My friend marks the sky like a pencil stroke, the far ridge is dark for her.

Speak to me out of that deep cavern, tell me
That the most intractable minute of all is coming;

That the air, steps of light, will pile higher than the edge of the cliff.

Alone by the Road's Edge

"You don't know what loneliness is until you've been left by the edge of the road, in the middle of nowhere, with nothing for company but a dancing chicken."
—Owner of a traveling animal show

The myth-maker drags his myth
Legs tethered together, squawking in chicken,
Down the cold nightroad unrolled
Into a world of rabbits.

Behind him the table-square mountain
Creases in jet-frost flakes; his own
World used to be bright and forward, his
Green suit smelled of candy

And his mother was a waitress named Helen.

Past every quartz rock he goes, flat lake soaked in stars,
To a restaurant named EAT. He'll wrench melodies out of the percolator,
Old crag of counter, streaked like jade,
House where all hopes come down. The performing egg
Glitters its wildest gold. Reflects

Memory's cozy auditorium hung with cellophane
In Hamtramck, Michigan.
Hordes of flash-toothed people there
Clap the roof down, wipe out the white odd desert;
Fill up our ears with clamor, wild acclaim

Applause for the magic-maker's heaven bird,
Its harsh dance, its grave eccentric song.

A Landscape Never Explored

It stretched out before us, a vast yellow plain, our lives would unroll there
Safely, in seas of wheat marbled by wind, in rivers of light;
Across it the marks of a great two-tracked reaper, in the distance
The city's heavy buildings.

You and I, two women, were going to travel it.
We would move in a series of cars,
In magic chess plays,
Always with someone else: a man to hold each of us around the waist,
Saying: there's the city; there's the way to reach it; there
Is a road as wide as the plains of the Bible.

Our figures would get lost in it; we'd merge into the horizon,
The sun softening our outlines,
Distant, gentle, just like everyone else.

We couldn't manage it,
Either of us, no matter how hard we tried.
No children around us like corn, ourselves not towers of corn,
No heavy sun
Pulling the love up out of the ground, sending it into

The growing yellow stands,
The ears of seed.

Vision of Bea

The railroad back to you runs only infrequently.

I've left you in a chair in a grand store,
Seated at a table clutching a glass,
A smile on your face. I think, she's gotten frailer over these years,
She's even had griefs in that other life.

The journey back to you is dangerous: a jetty of crumbling dirt;
I clutch a string for a guide. The railroad cars are too high to climb into,
They may not get me to you in time,
And rumor says someone was shot in that department store.

I keep trying, through webs of memory,
Through those last weeks of your life when you lay on the white bed
Holding your sister's hand,

Staring out, past the coughing machinery, the smoke-filled tunnel,
Clear to the air, the view, where
You, in a mirrored room
Nestle my past in your lap, under the shadow
Of your feathered hat.

In Mexico: The Indian Woman

Sits on the pavement, her back as straight as a door.
She stares at my feet; she works magic
With pyramids of peaches, moves them
Like counters in a game, like moving me.

The street cries, Ai! I think it slides
Toward that wide green gulch
That splits all of Mexico. The heavy buildings sag,
Light slides off the opera-house steps,
Guadalupe's courtyard crimps like an old gray grave, spouting
Red and blue brick, dust solid as chalk, jade sticks carved into
God's necklace, stumps of hands, nuts of heart;

The Tiffany roof of our hotel
Folds like an insect, sends
Pieces of glass, orange and blue arrows, home into me.

My kind left blood in their canals;
It marks there still, rust stains as high as a woman's hand.
The watcher with peaches shifts her topmost fruit, a gold keystone,
She doesn't tell me whether or not she knows,
We never speak.

We Live in the Ice Country

The earth's crust is bright blue, smooth to the hand,
Seven years' toil won't hack a hole through it
Although hell is straight down,
The palace of the king of darkness hung with gold plates,
And speckled hands of his enemies, tied up by their sinews.

Life on the surface is holiday.
Coins that fall from your pockets slide for miles,
Your breath flakes against your nose,
The people's eyes are round; they've straight white hair;
They're sewed into furs.

They pay no attention to rumors
Of splits in the ice, men coming out crooked as derricks,
Men with bleared eyes, breath stinking, damp,
The handles of their axes tagged with soft pale hair.

Visitors to Northern countries see
Hills and valleys smoothed out of ice,
Glass spires and huts, people in soft skin boots,

And a sheen across the glazed sky
Like the bottom of a pot.

Survivor

Even his iced-over nostrils, even
The mouth with its core of silver, the belly
Under the ice that's crazed in an Aztec pattern

Left a million years ago. His image
Has grown a crust of solitude like glass,
Layers of atmospheric salt,
Space weighing into the bottom of a pyramid,
Signals guarding in stripes of unbleached sound.

Inside, he's new. He'll surprise you all.
His skin is curled like a clenched leaf;
He has damp bland eyes; they'll dry to a china white,
And his mind holds

What any of us who've been frozen solid can tell you:
The shard of ice in the brain
Makes pictures brighter than death.

Threatened

We sit in a circle.
There are moving places in the floor, cracks
Which will grow to the sticky banks of a vast lake.

That young woman over there, clenched inward, she knows about this.
Her bones are harsh after nights on a pumice pillow,
Blankets that scratched her throat,
Night's dragonflies that sting and sting.
Her panic will sink us all, draw up
Bubbling stuff until it fills the room,
Pushes ahead of it our jackets, our wrenched-off shoes.

Where is the healer for her aching powers?
You whose wrists hurt, you with the pulse thudding underneath each ear,
You, young woman, with your cruelties, we can't reach out to you,
Our arms are glued to our sides, our
World tilts like a great dark melting plate.
The forces you've called in move among us, battered shapes,

They hold us apart,
They push us with their lumbering aimless shoulders.

Victim

Don't offer us grocery lists of reasons, don't
Appeal to us, ask us to fight each other.
What we want from you is simple: a splash of blood on the altar;
We'll mourn afterwards like bereft Arab women,
Toss ourselves onto the stone;
But don't be real. Your blood is not supposed to be sticky.

Because, if you say things like, wait for me, look at me,
You awaken the listener in us,
Who has to remember you're human,
That your hand shakes because the base of the temple is crumbling,
That the flick in your eyes is terror, old friend, old lover,
That the reflecting surfaces around you
Give back in sequence

Your face, our faces,
Our fears,
Like an advertising sign, like the machine they write heartbeats on
The one that measures
How to hold on.

Illinois Central Hospital

For Seth

Everywhere I go I have the sense
Of two arms around my ribs, a head under my chin; it feels like
A frightened child or an animal.

And I think of you, crouched asleep on two chairs
In a green hospital waiting room;
The squeaky waxed floor, the whispers, your son in his nest of tubes.

And I keep wanting to send you a telegram, a passport to a new country
Cut out of the seam of my arm.

I carry and soothe my tenant, its hand at my rib, the thumb
Tight against serrated skin,
The palm no bigger than an oak leaf.

Is there a comfort in carrying something? It's with me in your
                                    vinyl corridors; it's heavy
Like the last stages of doubt; it changes my shadow; it alters

The way I want for you, the way I walk.

The Sea Creature

It returns blinded in the night,
Cries outside my door:
Let me in;
You made me, seal's sleek fur, brain
That steered me back to you, blind in the dark, worm
Nudging doorsteps with my nose: this one, this one,
Then finally, familiar entrance, the way loved.

Lost in a dark world, jaws grinning,
Water crusted on my pelt;
Your empty spaces, human being
Are grown together in a barbed-wire hedge.

The animal used to be a sea creature.
It turns its life's compass westward,
It will send itself out over water like an oiled boat

Leaving me and my empty house appalled.

I'll lean my forehead on the windowsill, let the dust scrape me a
                                         headband,
Hating my year's harvest, rumpled empty bed,
A book on the floor, nothing to hold.

Out on the beach, the water settles shelf by shelf,
And the shadow of a vast wave raises, its top cut into bright green teeth.

House

Erased off the face of my earth, all that remains is a white space,
On it the possible ghost
Of roofline, window. I travel
Looking for myself in all the empty rooms
That say, why did you leave us.

Country of no-one. An open door, a dropped book, a photo of me at the
age of four.

I wait for myself on the stairs,
Touching a hand along the walls,
Move up behind myself, saying: Stop that.

In the upstairs room is the memory of another solitude; it once
Made a bright oxygen that raised my ribcage,
Touched against the insides of the windows, glowed out,
Filled up the whole house

To roofline, timbers, where now my own ghost climbs,
And the sparrow swings in under the roof ridge
Her wings beating
Searching for something she's hidden there.

The Child at the End of the World

Stop being here at the end of the world.

There's no room for children, solemnly watching
While the sky opens its shell,
Crust from a biologist's saucer.

Child, you can't have this time when the black shapes come home
Into their box that we kept the weights for living in;
Metal explores our street where the trees meet in the middle,
Streamers gout the branches.

While this heavy air waits, my calendar reminds: minutes
To recapture old losses,
Wrongs blurred as the morning paper,
Sleeps,
Whatever made that seam across the sky.

The child stares, green air etched on each eye.
He moves his feet on the burned stone and asks questions.

The cords on the back of his neck are crisp, like fuchsia stems.

Living on the Earthquake Fault

It zigzagged
Under my house, across the back of my garden
And into the hill. The tunnel to Solano Avenue
Cried tears out of the middle of the earth.
And I was the one who tried to hold it together. I grabbed like a clutching
                                                    grandmother,
Bridged the earth-slip with my spine.

When they said: let go, I said
I'm holding the world shut all by myself, soon
It will mend like a slit in an orange.

It takes time to learn the logic of chaos.
The open fissure
Ground up pebbles green as the coast of Ireland
Or streaked with blue like the bay, it spat out
Pieces of colored fire. My house sagged and squeaked. I went to look at
                                                    the view. It was
Extraordinary.

A vast new country, scarves of dark brown water,
It waited for me; it wanted my books and my children's mother;
It needed its name, and only I could say it.

Growing Coal

You and I don't matter in this situation, what matters is
That a family of four in a blue pickup truck
Will die on the freeway tomorrow afternoon.

Listen. There's a stretch of country outside the Coachella Valley
Where nothing has grown since the Pleistocene Era. They find there
Skeletons of big bony lumberers.
We're living in their graveyard, trying to grow something.

Back in the valley they have grapefruit big as your head;
Their children skip to school;
All we can grow is pebbles, coal watered with salt, clumps of sand.

You say, surely it will grow if we sing to it.
But sing your way to the last judgment and back, darling, darling;
That notion is childish.

The dinosaurs have left a spoor of droppings like petrified trucks;
Their stupid cunning is enduring as oil;
It snags the feet of the winged lizards,
The only desert creatures that can fly.

The Worst Motel

Advertises our ache in colored lights. It sends out
Beams into whatever country
We lay our road across. The worst motel draws us like fish-eye;
It drags us flat along its wide hard beds, its rock-red carpet;
It rinses us limp under its blind hot showers, it
Doesn't restore us ever. All the old aches
Are bluer than copper against our ribs,

And our eyes are rusty after a night of dreaming
About that other motel that hides outside our headlights. It would signal

Here's the real place to stay, with the oak doors.

Here is the sign that opens them, beyond that is a green courtyard, water
And a place to lean back, and words that you thought you had lost.
They wait there still, just spoken
Under the archways, over the grass.

Besieged

The bed was a dark blue raft
That turned in a tide that neither of us could measure.
Dangers paced us from the shore.
Help me, I said, and you couldn't hear because
The pictures on the shore were caverns to suck us under,
Oily swirls without bottom,
Diseases sent across on the fog in a conical
Dispersion. I can't hear you; your words make
A clatter against my life.

The walls of the room bleached pale; the bed
Swirled up to the waterfall.
The noise, I cried. I put my head under the pillow
And felt you floating away from me, far on a tide

Like an awkward movement of the planet, like the slow toppling of a cliff.
And there was no motion in your arm.

Cars Go by Outside, One After Another

I find it unbearable
That my hands should reach out for you, that I should see you
Retreating before me like a headlight beam along a ceiling

At night in a dark motel room. The bed's pillows
Are ranged around us, rocks at a cross-roads,
I hold out my hand;

I'm the woman in that dream about running.
My feet are grown into hedge-roots against the bed;
My fingers sprout brambles;
I can't ask you whether you'll stop or not;

You leave me
Like a searchlight ray, climbing the wall,
Slowly at first, then spreading awry,
Losing the power of light, losing the power of touch, dropping the edge

That might have controlled
Our night.

An Isthmus in the Bay

In a rigid, uninhabited country. No shelter at the end,
The corners of all objects hard;
Buildings stretch out to the skyline. The road
Is marked with grids. The traveler can move a square at a time.
But in the end his country is none;
And the road goes over the edge like a folded blanket.

We were two enemies kissing
On a California beach. The waves
Slipped gently near our feet.
It was more than I could bear. I drove off in my yellow car,
Thinking pain like a slash across a vacant landscape.

The water comes in slowly at Point Pinole.
The kissing lovers are islands under the ice-plant bank,
And I had schemed to put my body between you and tides of
Whatever: monsters, speckled, dim,
Strangers waiting for you on other beaches,
Death some day on an iron bed, no one to pull the shade.

The sea couldn't tell us enough. The light inside its crystal
Smashes into splinters of spray, leaving

No relic
Only spill upon the water.

Maude's Bar

Like the flash of heat across the face of the building,
Like the big drum, like the horn
That crawls up the side of the wall,
Yells at the center of my question,

Like the waiting that climbs on the wheels of clarinet,
Dances itself dizzy, breathes
Fire across the front of the building,
Over my life, where the ashes are. Fingers of flame tipped by ash
Rise over the roofs of San Francisco, outline
The tower with its praying mantis feet,

You with your long dark hair swinging over your shoulders:
"Every night for three months I went dancing; I couldn't sleep."

Halfway to the middle of the bay the tide turns over;
The sullen inshore current rushes out the Gate,
An implacable river of lighted water;
The colors of our scene run into each other.

The noise presses a drum against the wall; the heavy room
Is filled to its corners with you.

Are You Concerned for Your Safety, Alone in the House?

I'd welcome an intruder as specific as that:
Two large leather feet,
Beer on the breath, the pebble of stubble across the chin.
I'd be brave, crash through his stare, kick, bite,
Throw the heavy glass vase.

And no one would know about the body settled across my life like
                                                            furniture,
Curing me of those rooms alone,
The acres of pale floor, boards polished, windows bright,
Shining back my own composed face.

There are actions that turn your eyes gray in a night,
Change the way you breathe,
Make your wrists thicker. After that I'll be
The animal blocking the mouth of its cave,
The traveler at the edge of the forest

Preparing to walk all night.

Ship Wreck

Like that huddle of shape in the bottom of our own half-life,
In water more simple than the water it died in;
It calls at night,
The first of our losses,
Pulls at our air, makes our dark liquid, says

Twenty-five years it held the water apart with its bones.

The wanting stopped up my throat
With sand, coral, it grew
A cordon of beads that sewed my eyelids shut.
It drowned me again and again.

Can I remember a voice
Talking across Januarys?
The tides rise higher than our chins, signaling

That day when our whole world will be sea, our eyes be filled with water,

Homes for each other's questions.

January Class:
It Hasn't Rained for Seven Months

We dip into books as if they were
Wells of pity, cups of
Futures, lendings of light from the genuine owners of light,
Shining for miles into the awful garden
Where, deep enclosed, is the Rajah's frightening jewel.

In California almost everyone is divorced.
The eyes of my class stare at the pine tree that scrapes the building.
The clearing has in it your face, my face, the eyes
Of students bruised by the blue air of this
Driest January ever.

The sun comes through the window in knife patterns,
And none of us can say how it happens,
That loving turns to shapes so fierce,
Aiming for the lids, the corners of lips,
Wedging the voice. The edges of heat are square. They stop the throat.

But the jewel in the garden pulls like rain. Can it open
Our hard blue sky, can it
Make us speak.

IV

In the Basement of my First House

The child at the end of that passageway
Is a little monster waiting for
My flashlight beam, my hand to untie her, my voice to ask

The questions that she knows all the answers to. How long?
        Nights as dark as the bottom of a sack.
How much did it hurt? Forever.

She needs a bath, all that she's good for is talking;
I always knew they would leave you, she says.

I stare at my clean white hands.
There's no place under them for this
Morsel, snag-toothed urchin. This remnant of me.
The child has a difficult accent. I hate the scars on her ankle.

Outside of the window is a long blue plain, a sea as vast as the Sea of Azov,
Only fifteen feet deep at its deepest part.

They've gone away in a boat, the child says.
I always knew they would.

Recluse

The windows are hooded with iron,
And I'm inside, my white hands and face, my shreds of hair lost to the sun,
The air around my tower a frantic protection,
Birds fall headlong out of my sky,
Ivy leaves swell and explode,
And the bells of my tower sound warning,
Warning.

You can't reach me. Light would wilt my face like a leaf,
Turn the walls of my room into powder, nothing
That the hand could hold, an ash rising to choke your windpipe, coat
                                                    your heart
With a layer of clinging paper,

And scatter me, dust,
Across your foreground, in grains, in crying.

Iron house,
With its bird frozen solidly north,
That's me. But listen to the sound of my bells
Pulling birds out of the sky, forcing flight
Out of their plunging, forging it
Into a center of brass, into
A breaking, a broken
Echo.

Four A.M.

The walls of the room as far away as the south hedge of the garden,
Moonlight making your face on the floor,
I with my stomach in ridges, saying,
How will I live without wanting;

The button-molder can come in now
And simmer me down to lead,
My eyes, my fingers streamers of lead,
My chest a heavy bubble that two people can't carry.

Help me, anyone human,
Anybody who hasn't spent the night clutching iron.

The door opens; my son comes through it;
The heavy objects sag empty around him,
Your face is only a face again, or a pond of moonlight,
My bed is a bed like any other,
Outside the night relaxes,
The snail crosses the garden driveway
Leaving a bit of himself on each cast cement plate.

And the executioner packs up his melted metal,
His end of the world made into a cube,
His bucket of anger too heavy to lift.

Our World, and Us, Remade by Heat

The sky is broken into three charred pieces.
Buried somewhere in the place where they don't meet
Is the other edge of the circle that we don't make;
Out there all possibilities are tripled; there's an end
That everyone feels they are meant for;
There are fields of fire

That blind our eyes from the inside, flow out
Streamers behind each ear,
Sear us into what we never were

In the days when we fought, toe to toe, along the stairwell carpet,
Words like a flight of insects settling on the ceiling.
I opened my blouse: Jesus' bleeding heart;
I opened my skirt: the icy witches' birthmark.
Each of us saw over a shoulder time stopping,
The world splashing us free,
And fire in every corner of the room.

Now, burnt dry,
Against the pane of stars that scours our sky from crown to crown,
We revolve slowly, bounded by each other,
Mute, in the dazzling garden.

Metastasis

The vine in the veins insidiously
Webbed: roots pushed down into the fingertips,
So that one day you wake up and all of you is blossom.

Alien, it paints your scenery in clinging leaves;
Pale green fear,
Sticky, a snail's trail behind you.
The soft normal stuff of breathing
Struggles in jungle, thinks one-word thoughts: sun, me.
It's bent on itself,
Fights toward water like a maniac.

No one but you with your need to be loved,
I with my grasping solemn as lead,
Can make a shelter against it. Vines cover the outside,
An arabesque of roots, tied chains at the paper-thin peak of our roof.

Hold me.
The stem leans over my face,
Turns its mouth to mine, breathes me in. It's pulling me
Headlong,
Ahead of you,
Into its country.

Anger

The words that come out of her mouth are sullen as metal;
Her eyes watch something behind me,
Over my shoulder, the ultimate enemy, that desecrator we all fear
It opens there like a tunnel of noise, gestures at her with its long thin
                                                       windy fingers,
It has just written her name
Upside-down on a yellow-stained wall.
She hates it.

And we're only secondary. Semi-transparent, subway windows,
Shapes rush by behind us,
The nightmare and all its frantic crew, noises, blasts that skim the ear,
A long bare soot-streaked space starred with bolts, the
Shriek as the rod approaches its shaft, the sullen
Dragging protest of the wheels. And no one can help her.

It's that same long emptiness we've all looked down.

It pulls her until the inside of her head is hollow,
Makes her bones grate noise.

And all she can do is wait.
The light finally flickers dully in the opening
And she'll emerge,
Limp as cotton, sorry.

Waiting for my Eyes to Open on Day

It dropped over my head like a helmet, plating the nose and the eyes,
Blocking the channel that music might travel on,
Around my head the clasp of an iron pot,
Smelling of metal,
Heavy, rusting.

Names that come through are echoing,
Names of storms, of planets,
Ghosts, pounding the flats of their palms on the iron,

To clatter and scatter downhill, aiming like lead for
The cliff, its rocks, an acre of noise.
They bring with them heavy, rounded dreams.

But I'm trying and trying to dream of you, with your wizard's spoon, with
your view of the lake,
With your spells to split metal.
Surely you'll make a spell for me now,
Say it in more than words.

The broken edges of iron are white; its texture is silver.

Night's End

A box with dry edges, there's no
Collar or ridge, joinings
Draw space into themselves, they
Spit out objects like peach stones, they're
Shiny as onyx, you can't see
Your pale face in those walls, they swallow light.

If I could stand up and open out the evening
Like a sharp can chiseled down the middle
It would spill me out into a space

Open, deserted, where banks of moss are piled in terraces
Against a milky sky.

Somewhere a line of marchers trudges over a shuttered bridge,
Their boots graze near my ear, they make complaints
Of creaking bridge ties,
They pull a tired walker, his feet scraping behind him.

I'll try to follow them down their slope of night,
A steep roof
With a slow slide to a shelf at the bottom

Where a woman is waiting, holding a cup of water.

The Place Where Dreams Stop

I don't dream about you any more. There are only
Forests, the path down the hill where the
Greenery surrounds my face, the heavy
Wood in which I mend my brittleness, where
If I'm supple enough I'll slip through
Into leaves at the bosom, leaves at the waist, a shirt of leaves
Feathering the knuckles of both hands.

And no figure of you, either younger or older, no
Face of yours with its gray wary eye, no
Hand that told me that my ribs were brittle wood,
No country of yours, with steep roadways, dust at the bottom.

Against my landscape your figure fades, sandy as sparrow feathers,
Your wary step as careful, as crackling. . . .

Summer ground is a place for sleeping,
Ten years curled on the green weeds, fir needles pricking the sleeve of my
dress,
No waking until my eye lenses also are painted green
Making a green sky flaming for me, whether watered or not.

And no longer any step, your step
Exploring with its shoe-soles my bridges of bone.

New Tenants

The new people in our old house
Have moved all the furniture; they've installed
Different children on the swings. They don't know

That the bedrooms are haunted with talking pictures,
The stairs matted with questions,
The wallpaper patterned with Mexican hands and hearts,
There, where that other handsome couple practiced judo,
Touched once, and an arm broke off like a matchstick.

People have died in every room of that house.
The new tenants
Walk through those bodies as if they were holograms,

While we stay outside in the garden, displaced
Down to the corner where the last circle of sun
Hides on the wall of Mr. Dolan's greenhouse.

We live there as simply as mice; we've no one left to murder.

V

After the Cataclysm

Behind the rubble of water and rock, the upended shards of the
avalanche,

Under the overhanging cliff,
In a house with its back to the waterfall,
All the waters of earth are awake at our feet,
All the fish of the air are making their cries,

The rain comes down like tomorrow; fog
Closes us in, the fireplace
Swallows every timber of our belongings;
No one ever knocks at the door, the water
Is a turmoil that pulls the
Sun off its cloud-covered route,
The upper sky out of its smear in the Milky Way,
Pulls the center loose, with a tearing of soft wet cords.

Behind us the fall, a white dripping panel
Captures our shadow;
We are the only breathing creatures.

Now we can love each other, we say;
Now we are finished.

Our long dank hair is heavy with water.

Watching

Turning toward you in this pale room
With your shoulders bent, your head ducked forward, that vulnerable
Film across the eyes, the shadow
Of everything I've been waiting for,

Love comes in to us, heavy and stale-winged, powder of dust upon its
                                                    feet, layers
Of waiting filling me up to the edges of my life; there's no corner
That doesn't have your cushioning in it.

The medium I move in, my need, a soft silk, the clinging
Air we breathe, the brooding
Of tents, heavy as low cloud, shapeless, surrounding,
All is our ache, made out of forbidden stuff.
Live in me, I say to you now.

Around us the weave of an indestructible listening,
Love, a dark heavy sister waits over us,
Her watching so strong it melts the backbone, brings
Our word out of its grave, its hair thick in dust, its dark eyes wild.

How to Forgive

By ripping it out, tossed flopping like a fish
Into the air of the Cumberland Gorge. It will spin
Like a hobbled bird, like an old bean bag,
Thud against the sides of the earth's crust,
Finally send up sprouts
Of artery, trees toward the light

That shape questions in plant-language;
Stop, have you seen the one with the other half
Of the map, the answer to the acrostic question,
The one who has my future in his ledger?

Blind as a bat in the country of the blind,
My sensors know only touch on touch,
But you with your needle-green eyes can watch me wondering

Whether to go back with me into our past,
Again over the path with the sharp stones, down into the ravine.

It thumps there like a train on a siding.
The right side is for feeling;
The left side is the one that
Thinks and thinks.

Metamorphosis

Pulling itself up out of the water with the silver water running off it,
And fragments of sea bottom. The creature has lain in the mud
Buried, all but its eyes on stalks,

Its belly clutched in a knot of waiting
For the echoing siren
That could wake the dark water, pierce down to the undersea cliff
Where clutched in the monster's body was the thought of all its opposites.

When you and I said goodbye
I went upstairs and looked in the mirror,
The light shone white through my cheekbones,
From now on, I said, everything will be different.

I waited for a dryness that would coat nostrils, powder eye rims,
For vast dry decks of sand,
Hills, brown as cotton pods,
Sun that would blow away into a powder of rust

Everything except the great agate eye,
And the knob of pale shell where the heart used to pump sea water.

Recovering

At that fourth state of consciousness we've scattered everything extra,
Our pictures of people in sun, our long red hair.
The sea at Carmel
Is given away, first to lovers, then to strangers.

We're dressed in white treebark; we're free of it all,
With two down-at-heel shoes,
A feeling across the back of the neck of silence,
And the tremor of waiting.

When the flood comes up as high as the foot of the hill,
Pushing the Ark ahead of it, the leaves are washed green,
The smell of bay, sharp as a cut on the finger
Will bring it all back,
Leaning hard on those nerve ends that never agreed to sleep.

Our children will recognize us again;
The sun force under our eyelids each morning
All its old pain of glories.

Exorcising Ghosts

Six people with faces like smooth plaster,
Nothing where their mouths should be, space where their eyes might be,
Blanks turned toward me. Written on them
Whatever it is I want not to know.

Age huddles behind those husks,
Theft, death, in a room with a party table set
For a family which watches me, thinking,
Take your hand off that doorknob,
What are you doing there, dreamy-eyed, dawdling?

If I conjure long enough, I'll know how to tell them:

You're as different from me as breathing from drowning.
I'm going out in that afternoon that makes circles on closed eyelids;
I'll fool around in my garden.
Dig the mildew out from the roots of the tulip tree;
Bruise my fingers,

And never think of you again.
You're old.
You can't help yourselves.
You aren't real.

Learning to Type

A laboratory chimpanzee has been taught to communicate by means of a symbol-keyed typewriter

The sign for anger could be a felled pine tree.
Arbitrarily, love is a glass of orange juice.

On this machine you can type only declarative sentences:
My eyes hurt;
I have two tears sliding down the ridges of my nose;
My father lies on his hospital bed. His eyes are open.

A chimpanzee has no voice-box
And a machine must teach it the difference between make and give.
Make me a heart for giving; give me time.

I am sitting now at a machine like a middle aged woman.
Its panel is intricate and garbled; there are symbols for leave-takings:

Pictures of the crowd praying outside the cathedral,
Of the red train moving slowly off down the station.

If I study long enough I can find out how:
Machine, make me fingers to manage the dangerous keys.

Reprieved

I don't have to go to jail, I said.
I was pruning the apple tree; the children were around me;
My crime seemed vague as rumor. It must have happened years ago,
Or not at all, or under water,

With the heart rising to choke the gullet
And I couldn't breathe, panic folding in on me like the iron maiden;
It was always four in the morning, the bed as rigid
As an up-ended iceberg.

I don't have to go to jail.
I waited for the vultures to fly away.
The clock wheeled down its message from Time: You get used to things,
Your stomach knits over.

The garden that had been blue with panic
Grew moss across it.
I see you there only sometimes,
Pacing the far end of the lawn near the crippled swing;

You smile at me forgetfully; you wear a flowered shirt.

After You're All in Bed

Here's the door where the outside comes in,
Its white borders frothing like water;
The murmur of your sleeping wraps my throat.

The three of you in your badly made beds
Have left me alone with the fog swallowing the window-frame.
It speaks of you, of your hands unflexed on the pillow,
Trying to hold me, a globe with a future in it,
Flickering. There's my hidden city,
Its lighted distances; there's a street
That you could get lost in; there, at the core,
My final, irrevocable self,
A coal expanding, with a starred edge.

My gentle lover never prepared me for this.
He loved crowds, money, the smell of a warm fast train.

Tonight the air breathes, curved around the house.
The queen of silence, her knees bent, her head in fog,
Her calm hands spinning a heavy wool,
Is my reason tonight.

I open my mind to whiteness.

Home

Somewhere there's a street of empty houses,
Roof after roof, the doors bleached white by memory

Which I, like the force of night, travel over,
Making stairs out of words, sounds too low to hear.

Again and again in dreams, I
Find the right house, open the door. All that vanished furniture
Unreproachful, calls itself by the right names.
And the stream still runs down the gully; the old woman, leathery as a
bat,
Is dabbling her yellow toes in it.
We lead her home slowly in her damp print dress,

While down at the end of the street God still lives.
Our children play a high white noise at late o'clock;
We call to them, out on the porches, under the leaf-knobbed trees:
Come here, come back,
But the houses are as transparent as Corinth,

The beautiful roofline folds up into the sky
Closing us out.

Anima

But why are you sleeping, your wispy black hair
Touching your face in fern shreds, your eyes fringed shut, your own
Reflection painted below you, a reminder
Of something gone entirely away, my shadow's edge?

Because the dark-haired child that sleeps on the shelf over the pond
Must be my vanished mirror's face,
Jewels bloom around her, blue, green, hidden,
The water's as even
As a washed glass window. In it are pearls, ropy moss,
Feathered and dense, to climb higher than the ankle, glove the foot in
                                                              green fur.

I have always known her, a hidden listener, resting,
Living in this closed way. In her glass are jewels more variant
Than a maharanee's treasure, than all my hoardings;

Than the strange train of artifacts
Hiding, water-polished, under our sleep's blue shelf.

LIBRARY OF CONGRESS CATALOGING IN PUBLICATION DATA

Ó Hehir, Diana, 1929-
   The power to change geography.

   (Princeton series of contemporary poets)
   Poems.
   I.   Title.
PS3565.H4P6   811'.5'4   78-13323
ISBN 0-691-06385-0
ISBN 0-691-01354-3 pbk.